JOURNALING FOR 30 DAYS

Strengthening your Confidence
Self-Exploration and Development

Jan Mayfield

Journaling for 30 Days

Strengthening your Confidence

Self-Exploration and Development

ISBN: 978-1-8383132-0-3

Printed in United States of America.

Go Forward Fearlessly

Chapter title in "Inspirational Women of the World"

Journaling my way to freedom and growth!

This journal is deliberately black and white.

Add your kaleidoscopic colour to your life.

Keep on track, reflect and grow.

Live and love in life and business.

CONTENTS

PREFACE

Journaling for 30 days was born out of my passion for helping people to release from their past what they do not need in the present.

You'll hear people speaking about journaling very often. Some shun it away, stating that they would not know what to write.

Journaling with me takes away any fears you may have about what to write; this is not a diary of events in your life. Rather, it's a way of painlessly extracting stuff you have buried in your subconscious mind and being able to see your full potential.

To be in touch with all sides of you as a person, to connect to soul and the reason you are on earth, to me, is imperative if you want to live the best version of you. This journal will encourage you to do just that. Focusing on other areas which may or may not turn out to be problematic will help you to release what does not serve you currently.

If your business, personal and spiritual lives are in full flow, then perhaps this journal is not for you.

It is for you if you know there is more to life than the one you have. If you are stuck and stagnant in certain areas, then this will unstick you and bring forth flow. This journal, if done for 30 days, will release you from some old habits and give you that wonderful sense of wanting to carry on and move forward to receive your magic.

As a result of journaling with me, you will create a thirst for life, know what you can achieve beyond what you think you can at present and learn to trust in YOU.

NOTES ABOUT YOUR JOURNALING

After seeing the success of my mentees on their journaling journey, I must give you the opportunity for that success too.

Journaling gives you a daily focus and helps to eliminate habits that no longer serve you. It subtly extracts what you do not need to focus on and raises your platform of inspiration to embrace life.

In life, it is important to create a space for you, a space to connect to. I call it the universal energies, but you can say God, Angels, Divine, energy, or whatever your 'thing' is.

You are connecting to a hidden steering column which takes you in the right direction when you fully engage your gears!

"...Life is much easier as a result of journaling..." JB *"I would recommend anybody that's on their journey to connect with Jan; she is a great mentor."* JB

WORDS FROM PREVIOUS JOURNALING MENTEES

Journaling my way will bring out the best in you, and as you can see from these five ladies' experiences, everyone is different.

I have discovered a deeper understanding of my life and the way I view life as a result of the questions Jan gives us to journaling posts. I had to dig deep to find some of the answers and some were quite confrontational when I dissected the answers, and in that right there I found the answers to some of my personality-forming characteristics that I had wondered about – xx.

—Jacqueline Obrien-Langan, Ireland

It gave me focus; me time also challenges me to come out of my comfort zone to grow. Some things I thought I could not do surprised me also when I did do them. Journaling has been a very positive experience, even though sometimes I may feel I don't want to do a task. It's been a good motivator for me and something I look forward to, to see what journaling has for me each day.

—Dianne Lawson, UK

Journaling has made me face myself. I have discovered that even though I may be able to alter or lessen what I may say depending on who I'm talking to when it comes to the written word, all that I think and feel is freely and honestly expressed. The pen is mightier than the sword, but especially so when it is your pen, about yourself. It is one of the most helpful, enlightening and therapeutic things that anyone can do to achieve an understanding of what life is about.

—Bambi Franklin, Ireland

If journaling is something you have not tried, it's definitely worth the effort. It may seem like work initially but then it just starts to flow—when you ask the universe to "give me the words to write," you can absolutely surprise yourself with the beautiful things that can appear on the page.

In the long run, you get much more out of it than you have put into it.

It is a reflection of you, a reflection of your spirit, of your heart… And a way of thanking the universe for all that you have in this life.

—Laura King, USA

"Releasing, awakening, relieving, calming."

—Laura DS

HOW TO USE YOUR JOURNAL

Be sure to read this page and use it as a reference

◊ Have a notebook or journal to use alongside this book and write directly into the book.

◊ Coloured pens and pencils are essential.

◊ Begin at the beginning - day one is day one - try not to miss a day. Day one begins at the end of the day in this set of journaling.

◊ When I mention Universe or universal-energies, find your words if this does not resonate. I am talking about anything that is not earthly.

◊ Be comfortably uncomfortable with some of the journaling days - it is good to find your inner workings.

◊ You might be asked to feel something - do this by taking at least 4 deep breaths in and 4 exhales with your eyes closed - allow yourself to relax and feel a connection to you.

◊ Use the breathing before you begin most days if you wish; it will give you a different perspective.

◊ Be honest - dig deep for some answers - take the first words that come to mind, too.

◊ When you are asked to say something - you can also write it in your journal.

◊ I talk about the human you and soul you - this is thinking as you (human you) and thinking with the breath connection (soul).

◊ I will also talk about your subconscious mind; think of this as a place where all your experiences and emotions are stored from when you were in the womb.

◊ Speak out to the universe: say a little mantra in your head or, better still, out loud.

◊ Examples of mantras are at the back of the book.

◊ I may ask you to look for signs in your life. These can be anything from words, repetitive actions, colours, sounds, songs, connecting to names and people, plus much more.

◊ This journal will become a masterpiece; 30 days of your life in words and colour.

REFLECTION

The following pages have space for reflection on each journaling day.

Sometimes we have an outstanding moment of release or change. That 'Ah-ha' moment needs to be logged before it leaves us. You may have a profound dream with content that you just do not want to forget.

Log it here.

Use reflection in any way that suits you; there are no rules.

Recognise any patterns that have emerged throughout the days of journaling and the reflective diaries.

◊ What repetitions have you observed?

◊ What flowed?

◊ What did not flow?

◊ What is flowing now?

◊ Have you noticed changes in any areas of your life?

◊ How do you feel?

◊ What is your temperament now?

◊ How are your emotions?

◊ Do you have or have you lost any cravings?

◊ What are you ready to action?

◊ Anything else?

JOURNALING DAYS

Leave a trail of happiness in the footsteps of your journey.

DAY 1

REFLECTION

1. What happened today? Write about it.

a. Think about today and write down all your positives and negatives.

b. What would you change?

c. What would you leave as it was?

2. Speak out to the universe about how grateful you are for everything today. Say thank you.

3. Say and write 11 times:

"I am ready to fill tomorrow with abundance."

REFLECTION

EMOTIONS:

THOUGHTS:

TO DO:

1.____

2.____

3.____

4.____

5.____

Lucid are your dreams yet to unfold.

DAY 2

CONTOURED

1. Select one of the negatives from yesterday and think about how you can flip it to a positive. What changes do you need to make?

2. Say and write 11 times:

"I am created as an illuminated being."

3. Sit down with a piece of paper and coloured pencils. Begin to sketch, colour, draw, etc.

Allow your creativity to flow!

REFLECTION

EMOTIONS:

THOUGHTS:

TO DO:

1.____

2.____

3.____

4.____

5.____

Eruptions of ideas; select what are true for you.

DAY 3

DASHING

1. Look in the mirror - what do you see?

a. Journal all that you see, think and feel.

2. Say and write the following 11 times:

"I have all that is, to be all that I am."

3. What do the following mean to human you and soul you?

Prize, Fresh, Atmospheric

Write from your soul (connect to the inner you) and human you for your words.

____

____

____

____

____

____

____

____

REFLECTION

EMOTIONS:

THOUGHTS:

TO DO:

1.____

2.____

3.____

4.____

5.____

Let the curls unfold as the vacuum of presence is released.

DAY 4

SUPER

1. Thinking about the last 3 months, how have you transitioned in that time? What is different and how have you evolved?

2. Say and write 11 times:

"Gratitude is something I practice every day."

3. Write from your soul (inner you) or from your heart; whatever comes forward. Try not to think too much and allow your pen to do the work.

REFLECTION

EMOTIONS:

THOUGHTS:

TO DO:

1.____

2.____

3.____

4.____

5.____

Solid are the moments; sit and contemplate, but not for too long.

DAY 5

DANCING

1. Listen to the signs you are given in life. What do you think stops you from recognising and taking action?

2. Write and say the following 11 times:

"Love, is love for and of everything."

3. Your inner self (soul) has a message for you - listen and write your personal message.

REFLECTION

EMOTIONS:

THOUGHTS:

TO DO:

1.____________________________________

2.____________________________________

3.____________________________________

4.____________________________________

5.____________________________________

Solid are your foundations; insecurity and disharmony are there to create instability. Know your structure.

DAY 6

CONTENTMENT

1. Today I would like you to think of something you want to manifest. Something that you would like in your life.

2. Write in as much detail as possible - what you see, sense, smell, colours, size - get pictures. Breathe it!

3. Write and say the following 11 times:

"I can, I am, I do."

REFLECTION

EMOTIONS:

THOUGHTS:

TO DO:

1.____

2.____

3.____

4.____

5.____

Receive the healing as your thoughts create reality.

DAY 7

EXCITED

1. Look at yesterday's manifesting and add some more detail today to help it to grow. Water the seeds you are sowing in your life's manifestation.

2. Think about a skill that you want to share or use to develop part of your life or business. Write what this is.

3. Spend time writing 10 steps to achieve number 2.

4. How are you going to use that skill?

5. Say and write the following 11 times:

"I have all the skills I need. I can access all that I need. I am allthat I need."

REFLECTION

EMOTIONS:

THOUGHTS:

TO DO:

1.____

2.____

3.____

4.____

5.____

Tread where the trodden have not ventured.

DAY 8

BELIEVE

1. Continue with your thoughts on manifesting - shout it out to the world, sing it, dance it, write it!

GET EXCITED

2. Throughout today, spend time thinking about your manifestation and visualise that you have it, you can have it and it will be yours.

Believe it!

3. Write in your journal and say the following 11 times:

"The timing is right."

REFLECTION

EMOTIONS:

THOUGHTS:

TO DO:

1.____

2.____

3.____

4.____

5.____

Diamonds and guides spread the sparkle for you to walk into.

DAY 9

DIAMOND

1. How is your manifesting coming along? How are you feeling?

2. What do you think about genius?

3. Are you a genius? Does everyone have the potential to be? Write about this.

4. Write in your journal and say the following 11 times:

"Thank you; I am grateful."

REFLECTION

EMOTIONS:

THOUGHTS:

TO DO:

1.____

2.____

3.____

4.____

5.____

Rocky is the road; see the strength within today!

DAY 10

EXPRESSION

Get creative! (If you have never done this before, then now is the time to start!) E-mail me a copy of your work of art if you wish.

Draw, stick, cut, paint, colour...what is your creative?

REFLECTION

EMOTIONS:

THOUGHTS:

TO DO:

1.____

2.____

3.____

4.____

5.____

Crispness, white and sharp inventiveness bring those keys for success.

DAY 11

TREASURE

1. Time to be a little analytical today.

2. Look at your artwork from yesterday.

3. Take note of the colours and shapes you have used; compliment yourself on how creative you are.

4. Share it with a friend or me.

REFLECTION

EMOTIONS:

THOUGHTS:

TO DO:

1.____

2.____

3.____

4.____

5.____

Boldness and resolution are the keys.

DAY 12

DIVINE INTELLIGENCE

1. Check in with your manifesting - do you have any results yet?

2. I hear the word FRESH - what does your soul (inner self) energy say about it?

3. It is time for some gratitude write and say - 10 things you are grateful for from last week.

4. Someone has written a song for you. What is the name of it?

REFLECTION

EMOTIONS:

THOUGHTS:

TO DO:

1.____

2.____

3.____

4.____

5.____

Draw on the symbols; create a little diversion to eliminate self-destruction.

DAY 13

PRAISE

1. Reflection time. What have you experienced that is new in the last 7 days?

2. I hear the word OPEN - what does your soul/inner self energy say about it? Write at least 3 paragraphs.

3. It is time for some ACKNOWLEDGEMENT - acknowledge and accept your positive traits by writing them down.

4. Write and say the following 11 times:

"I shine my beauty from within."

REFLECTION

EMOTIONS:

THOUGHTS:

TO DO:

1.____

2.____

3.____

4.____

5.____

Pure magic is the path you travel to your destiny.

DAY 14

SUCCESS

1. Think about yesterday's acknowledgement of new things in your life.

How did you find this? What areas were more difficult? Write about this from your heart.

2. Imagine you are a plant! Write about how you feel being sown into the earth to begin the plant journey and follow through to blooming.

3. Write and say the following 11 times:

"My inner guidance is all I truly need right now."

REFLECTION

EMOTIONS:

THOUGHTS:

TO DO:

1.____

2.____

3.____

4.____

5.____

Sense the virginity, the newness of every day.

DAY 15

FLOWING

1. Think about someone special in your life. What words do you use to describe your relationship with them?

2. Think about beauty; what is beauty to you?

3. Write and say the following 11 times:

"I stop procrastinating, now!"

REFLECTION

EMOTIONS:

THOUGHTS:

TO DO:

1.____

2.____

3.____

4.____

5.____

Breathe in the light of life, breathe out the depths of despair.

DAY 16

FORWARD

1. Jump in with both feet! Yes, it is time to find something new and ACTION IT.

2. Take time today to think about something you have been wanting to do for a while. Write the steps needed to begin it. Think it, feel it, know it.

3. Write and say the following 11 times:

"I am recognising what I know I need to do."

REFLECTION

EMOTIONS:

THOUGHTS:

TO DO:

1.____

2.____

3.____

4.____

5.____

Stop and think. What do you think? Wait for the ideas and words to enter and act accordingly.

DAY 17

GRACIOUS

1. Think about what you are ACTIONING. What can you add to it and what do you need to take away?

2. Be concise and rather ruthless…imagine you are doing this for someone else.

3. Close your eyes and think about what you are actioning. How and where do you feel it in your body?

4. What colour and shape do you feel with this?

5. Write and say the following 11 times:

"I will not listen to human me for most of today."

REFLECTION

EMOTIONS:

THOUGHTS:

TO DO:

1.____

2.____

3.____

4.____

5.____

Love internally to form a barrier and create that empowering place of oneness.

DAY 18

RECOGNITION

1. How do you feel about your tasks over the last couple of days?

2. Move on a little now from your actioning; allow it to feed into your life and just let it be.

3. Write and say the following 11 times:

"I am delighted with my life."

REFLECTION

EMOTIONS:

THOUGHTS:

TO DO:

1.____

2.____

3.____

4.____

5.____

Be the chameleon; fuse with all situations to reveal optimum light.

DAY 19

JEWEL

1. Today is a good day to sort out and put things in place, both physical and mental. Dip into your life and file away, throw away and keep only the cream of the crop.

2. Draw a TREE – then decorate it as you wish.

3. Write and say the following 11 times:

"I am grounded and protected always."

REFLECTION

EMOTIONS:

THOUGHTS:

TO DO:

1.____

2.____

3.____

4.____

5.____

Blend with your emotions and emerge powerful.

DAY 20

HEART-FELT

1. Take time today to think about what uplifts you. Write about this in your journal.

2. Speaking to you as an 11-year-old, what would you say?

3. Write and say the following 11 times:

"I am LOVE."

REFLECTION

EMOTIONS:

THOUGHTS:

TO DO:

1.____

2.____

3.____

4.____

5.____

Grace and sincerity go together; bind them and feel a motivational presence.

DAY 21

BLESSINGS

Go outside and do what makes you feel connected to all that is.

Look at everything around you as though you have never seen it before.

Write and talk about your experience.

REFLECTION

EMOTIONS:

THOUGHTS:

TO DO:

1.____

2.____

3.____

4.____

5.____

Seldom do you not know what to do. Look in your heart and soul; this is where the answers reside.

DAY 22

FLY-FREE

1. Breathing: take time out today to practice buddha breathing.

2. Breathe in through your nose, deep into your belly - then out through your mouth, pushing your belly back to your spine as you empty the stale breath from within.

3. This will energise you!

4. Write a few words to describe your day today.

REFLECTION

EMOTIONS:

THOUGHTS:

TO DO:

1.____

2.____

3.____

4.____

5.____

Plunge into the depths, look for the light, see the way and ask to be guided.

DAY 23

SHARE

1. Take time today to share your words with others and have the intention to help them in their lives.

2. Endeavour to share small words; they can mean so much to someone. A smile, hello, or gratification to a stranger might be the only positive contact they receive.

REFLECTION

EMOTIONS:

THOUGHTS:

TO DO:

1.____

2.____

3.____

4.____

5.____

Forge ahead through the sea of blindness; your vision restores.

DAY 24

TRANSMUTATION

It is time to create a verse or two using some of the words below; create some form of poetry.

CONSUMMATE, REJUVENATE, SEEKING, PLEASURE, GAZE, STARLIGHT, EVENING, CONSTRUCT, SHARE, ENERGY, FOREST, DIAMOND, FRAGMENTED, DELIGHTFUL, DELIVER, ACTIONING, DANCING, LAUGHTER, CHERISH, FLOWERY, STIGMA, VISIBLE.

Allow your words to flow…

REFLECTION

EMOTIONS:

THOUGHTS:

TO DO:

1.____

2.____

3.____

4.____

5.____

You are here to celebrate! You have made another milestone.

DAY 25

DELIVERANCE

Gratitude day is here.

1. We must be grateful for all that we have, including the not-so-good times.
2. Today, take time out and be conscious that you are grateful for everything in your life.
3. Say it, feel it, sense it and know it!
4. How amazing do you feel today?

REFLECTION

EMOTIONS:

THOUGHTS:

TO DO:

1.______________________________________

2.______________________________________

3.______________________________________

4.______________________________________

5.______________________________________

Dive deep into the depths of the world's evolutions.

DAY 26

TRIUMPHANT

1. Clear your workspace - clear your drawers and throw away what is not needed.

2. Start to order your journals and other books that you write in. Consolidate as much as you can.

3. Write a few words at the front of each journal - wisdom.

4. Say and write 11 times:

"I am the love; I share this with others."

REFLECTION

EMOTIONS:

THOUGHTS:

TO DO:

1.____

2.____

3.____

4.____

5.____

Railway your tracks and lay them in place, ready for new transformation.

DAY 27

ANTICIPATION

1. You are in line for a gift over the coming few days - you will not know what this is.

2. Tell the universe you are ready to receive the gift it has for you - say thank you and see what materialises.

3. Think about it today then leave it to happen; forget about it!

4. Say and write 11 times:

"I am the blessings; I share these with others."

REFLECTION

EMOTIONS:

THOUGHTS:

TO DO:

1.____

2.____

3.____

4.____

5.____

Master the masterpiece; blank is the canvas to sketch your notions.

DAY 28

EMBRACING

1. Today, think about times when you may have been a little down and thoughts of unworthiness crept in.

2. When did this last happen?

3. What was it you thought you were not worthy of? Write in your journal as much as you can about this.

4. Say and write 11 times:

"I am worthy, now and always."

REFLECTION

EMOTIONS:

THOUGHTS:

TO DO:

1.____

2.____

3.____

4.____

5.____

Be divine and connect to your inner self, for there lay the answers you seek.

DAY 29

TOTALITY

1. Be grateful today for all that you have. Name 10 things you are grateful for in your life - not family and friends, please.

2. Look out of the window and write what you see. Look out of the window one hour later and write what you see, giving as much detail as possible.

3. Say and write 11 times:

"I have all that I need right now."

REFLECTION

EMOTIONS:

THOUGHTS:

TO DO:

1.____

2.____

3.____

4.____

5.____

Be attractive to the mirror as you love your reflection.

DAY 30

MAY YOUR NEW CHAPTER BEGIN!

Massive congratulations! You are on day 30 of your journaling journey.

Be incredibly happy with yourself and your achievements.

Reflect today and share what your highs and lows were on this journey.

You are on a high now, and the lows were a learning curve that has since melted into life.

Write and say the following 11 times.

"I am ready for my next 30 days of my journaling."

REFLECTION

EMOTIONS:

THOUGHTS:

TO DO:

1.____

2.____

3.____

4.____

5.____

MANTRAS

A mantra needs to be straight and to the point, with no waffling or negative words.

A GOOD MORNING MANTRA

Dear universal energies, please give me everything I need to be the best version of myself today. Thank you.

ASKING FOR WORDS TO WRITE

Dear universal energies, I am ready to write from my soul intuition. Please give me all that I need right now. Thank you.

Dear universal energies, please give me all that I need to know as I move forward in my life. Thank you.

Dear universal energies, I am ready to be shown a little more of my soul purpose. Please give me the words to write. Thank you.

A GOOD EVENING MANTRA

Dear universal energies, thank you for such a wonderful day, full of experiences that my soul needed to have. I am ready to release all that does not serve me for tomorrow. Thank you.

These are some of the mantras you are likely to need while journaling. If you are creating your own, make sure they flow like the ones above. It is ok to change the words universal energies to something else if you wish. For example, the name of your god.

Be consistent in all your mantras in the format and the time of day that you say them.

Relax, trust, and believe in all that you do.

As my recognised soul purpose becomes stronger by the year, I know I have to share with you in as many formats as possible ways in which you can help yourself to be the best version of you.

We are all here on this earth to connect to our soul and grow, to enjoy life and have magical times.

Sometimes, we need a little help.

Journaling is one way of easing that connection to our soul and its mission.

You have succeeded in these **thirty days of journaling!**

I say well done to all of you, and I am proud and excited for the next phase in your life.

You are now ready for more. Journaling done daily can only enhance and quicken your connection to true purpose. You may want to have a month off or connect to Journaling for Thirty Days, book 2.

The choice is yours. If you feel you are slipping in life or need an extra hand up, then get on your journaling again.

Personal development and growth are a continual process in your evolution.

ACKNOWLEDGEMENTS

I like to acknowledge those who have helped me in my life, being grateful and appreciative to all on my path for whatever reason you have been there – I thank you.

To the members of my online group Universal-Energies Life and Soul Purpose living, I thank you for embracing your uniqueness and delivering tasks so eloquently. Your passions grew as did your thirst for life and soul growth. I am proud to know all of you.

Bambi, Jacqueline, Dianne and Dianne, Rach, Laura and Laura for your honest feedback about your journaling experiences. I know it has made such a difference to your lives and has given new 'journalers' a window into your journaling.

ABOUT THE AUTHOR

Jan Mayfield is an inspirational speaker and author of Zoetic Soul: Pertaining to Life . Your Life. And co-author of Inspirational Women of the World, published in November 2020. Formerly a teaching and management professional, she switched direction - after experiencing a traumatic accident - to pursue her passion for understanding her soul's purpose in life.

Jan diligently rose from illness and began to release her true self using a sequence of coordinated events.

For almost three decades, she has been a successful entrepreneur and an intuitive coaching consultant.

Radiating warmth and compassion, this gifted, intuitive woman's unique approach brings insight and empowerment to her clients, offering them the opportunity to reach their souls' full potential.

"I just love how you combine your experience in the personal development industry with your spiritual teachings. The world needs more people like you, especially now..." Landi Jac, Global Director, Worldwide Business Intelligence.

www.janmayfield.com
www.universal-energies.com

FB Jan Mayfield and Jan Mayfield's page
IG Januniversalenergies
TT Januniversalpsychic
YT Jan Mayfield
LI Jan Mayfield

Books:
Zoetic Soul
Inspirational Women of the World co-author
Journaling for 30 Days

Printed in Great Britain
by Amazon

29378995R00066